GREAT WHALES
The Gentle Giants

Here's a list of some other Redfeather Books from Henry Holt

Snakes: Their Place in the Sun
by Robert M. McClung

*Something Special
by Emily Rodda

*Stargone John
by Ellen Kindt McKenzie

213 Valentines
by Barbara Cohen

*Weird Wolf
by Margery Cuyler

Available in paperback

GREAT WHALES

THE GENTLE GIANTS

Patricia Lauber

illustrated by

Pieter Folkens

A Redfeather Book

Henry Holt and Company // New York

Henry Holt and Company, Inc.
Publishers since 1866
115 West 18th Street, New York, New York 10011

Henry Holt is a registered trademark of
Henry Holt and Company, Inc.

Library of Congress Cataloging-in-Publication Data
Lauber, Patricia.
Great Whales, the gentle giants / by Patricia Lauber;
illustrated by Pieter Folkens.
(A Redfeather book)
Includes index.
Summary: Describes the characteristics and behavior
of different kinds of whales and discusses why they
are threatened by extinction.
1. Whales—Juvenile literature. [1. Whales.]
I. Folkens, Pieter A., ill.   II. Title.
III. Series: Redfeather books.
QL737.C4L283   1991
599.5—dc20   91-692

ISBN 0-8050-1717-8 (hardcover)
10 9 8 7 6 5 4 3 2
ISBN 0-8050-2894-3 (paperback)
10 9 8 7 6 5 4 3 2 1

First published in hardcover in 1991
by Henry Holt and Company, Inc.
First Redfeather paperback edition, 1993

Printed in the United States of America
on acid-free paper. ∞

This book is based in part on an earlier book by Patricia Lauber,
Great Whales (Garrard Publishing Company, 1975).

Contents

GREAT WHALES
The Gentle Giants

1 // *The Gray Whales*

Early each winter a parade of whales passes the west coast of North America. Traveling in small groups, thousands of whales swim south. In the water, powerful tails pump. Long, dark bodies glide forward in shallow dives. On shore, thousands of people turn out to watch the whales go by.

The passing whales are the kind called gray whales. They are some of the world's big whales. Adults may be 50 feet long and weigh more than 40 tons. Like all whales, they swim by moving their broad tails up and down. They steer with their flippers. Grays are not the world's fastest whales. But they are the champion long-distance swimmers. Every year they make a round-trip of perhaps 10,000 miles through the Pacific Ocean.

A gray whale spy-hops—pops up in the water to look around.

Gray whales spend the summer in the far north. The food-rich waters in and near the Bering Sea are their feeding grounds. There the whales feast on small animals of the ocean floor. They dive and surface, dive and surface. Like all whales, they must surface to breathe. Whales live in the sea, but they are not fish and they cannot take oxygen from water. Whales are mammals, just as we are. They take oxygen from air by breathing in.

While they are feeding, the gray whales build up a thick layer of fat, called blubber. During the rest of the year, they will eat little. Instead, their bodies will draw on the blubber for energy. Blubber also helps to keep the whales warm. It seals in the heat that their bodies make.

As summer ends, the gray whales head south toward warm waters. There calves are born and mating takes place. The whales that lead the way south are females that will give birth during the winter. For them there is no time to waste. Newborn calves have no blubber to keep them warm in cold water. The other whales follow. All are swimming at about four miles an hour.

By December the first whales are passing San Diego, California. They are nearing the end of their trip—the warm, shallow bays, called lagoons, of Baja California. In the far reaches of the lagoons, calves will be born during the next six weeks.

A newborn gray whale looks like its mother, except that it is smaller. Even so, it is a big baby. It is 12 to 15 feet long and weighs about a ton. It is born knowing how to swim.

Mammals nurse their young on milk. The gray whale nurses her baby by rolling onto her side and squirting milk into its mouth. The young whale feeds underwater, then surfaces to breathe. It has a huge appetite. A young gray drinks 50 gallons of milk a day.

During its first months, a calf never strays far from its mother. She strokes it with her

TWO SWIMMERS

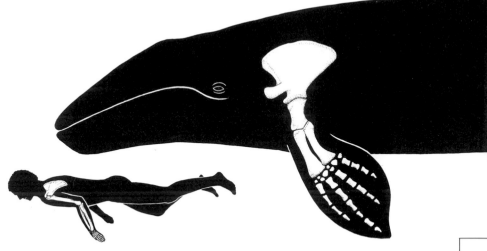

A 6-foot-tall swimmer is dwarfed by a small gray whale, about 23 feet long. This drawing shows how the bones in a whale's shoulder and flipper compare with the bones in a human shoulder and arm.

flippers. She plays with it. And she takes great care of it. A mother never leaves her calf on its own.

Each winter only some of the females have calves. The other females are with the males, in the open waters of the lagoons. For them winter is the time for being courted and mating.

The whales stay in the lagoons through

winter and early spring. They seem to have a very good time. They swim and roll. They ride the surf at a lagoon's opening. They spy-hop—popping up in the water and looking around. They dive and surface.

Before diving, each whale fills its lungs with air. It breathes through two blowholes, which are slits in the top of the head. The blowholes snap shut to keep out water.

When a whale surfaces, air rushes out of its lungs. The whale's breath is hot and moist.

As it strikes the air above the ocean, it is cooled. The moisture in it turns to little drops of water. The breath can then be seen. It looks like a spout of water. Often it is called a blow.

The blowing, leaping whales draw crowds of people. Some go out in small boats to be among the whales. And over the years, a strange thing has happened. In 1977 one gray whale in one lagoon allowed itself to be petted by people who were studying the whales from a boat. Somehow other whales learned about

A WHALE'S BODY

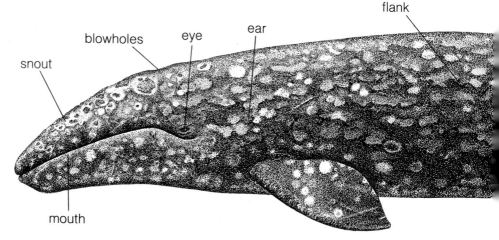

flank

blowholes   eye   ear

snout

mouth

this. Today they rush up to whale-watching boats to have their backs and heads rubbed. Some roll over for a belly rub. With a flick of its big tail, a whale could crush a boat. But the whales seem to be careful. They are friendly and they want to be stroked. They act like gentle giants. And the same thing seems to be true of other big whales, which are often called great whales. The name sets them off from smaller whales and their many close relatives.

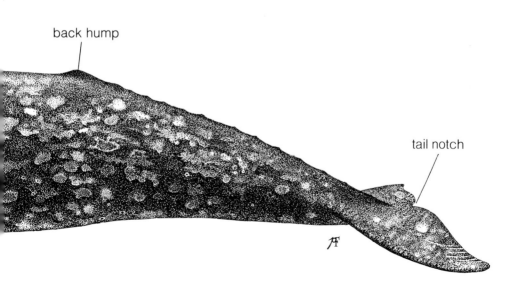

2 ∥ Sorting Out the Great Whales

To sort out whales and their relatives, scientists begin by dividing them into two main groups.

One group is called toothed whales. It is made up of whales with teeth and their close relatives, such as dolphins. All use their teeth to grasp their food, which they usually swallow whole. Most toothed whales eat fish, as well as squid, which are relatives of the octopus. A toothed whale has a single blowhole on the top of its head.

Most of the world's whales are toothed whales. And nearly all of these are fairly small. Only one is counted as a great whale. It is the sperm whale.

A blue whale, the largest animal on earth, surfaces and blows.

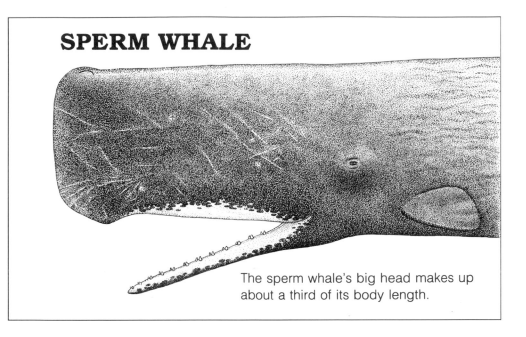

SPERM WHALE

The sperm whale's big head makes up about a third of its body length.

A sperm whale is easy to tell from other whales. It has a huge, squared head. The teeth of this big whale are in its lower jaw. They are some of the biggest teeth on earth, each the size of a man's fist. The whale may have as many as 50 teeth, which it uses to seize its prey. Its chief prey are squid. Some of them are longer than the whale itself.

Whales in the second main group do not have teeth. Instead, each has what looks like a huge mustache growing from the gums of its upper jaw. The mustache looks hairy, but it is not made of hair. It is sometimes called whalebone, but it is not made of bone either. It is made of the same sort of material as our fingernails. The best name for it is baleen.

A baleen whale has several hundred tightly packed blades of baleen. The outside of the baleen is smooth. The inside edges of the blades are fringed. Whales use their baleen to strain tons of tiny sea animals out of the water.

All the baleen whales are counted as great whales, even though some of them are fairly small. Scientists divide them into families.

The biggest family is made up of the whales called rorquals. The name describes a whale with a small fin on its back and a throat with deep pleats. When a rorqual gulps a giant mouthful of water and food, the pleats in its throat expand like the pleats in an accordion. Muscles in its belly and jaws tighten. Water is pressed out, but food is trapped by the baleen.

Like other whales, rorquals feed on small sea animals. They often eat krill, which look

HOW A RORQUAL EATS

As a rorqual gulps water and food, the pleats in its throat expand.

like tiny shrimp and are found near the surface. Some also eat schools of small fish.

The biggest family of whales holds the biggest animals ever to live on earth. These are the blue whales, which are larger than the largest dinosaurs were. A blue whale is so big that it is hard to imagine. Fully grown, it is longer than four buses placed end to end. Its heart is the size of a small car. Its tongue weighs as much as an elephant. It eats two tons of food a day. A newborn calf is as much as 25 feet long, weighs seven and a half tons, and drinks 100 gallons of milk a day.

The next-biggest whale is also a rorqual: the fin whale. It is slightly slimmer and more streamlined than a blue whale.

The sei whale, Bryde's whale, and the minke whale are also rorquals. Not much is known about them. The sei is probably the fastest swimmer of all whales, reaching speeds of 25 miles per hour. Minkes are the smallest of the rorquals. Like dolphins, they swim

THE GREATEST OF THE GREATS

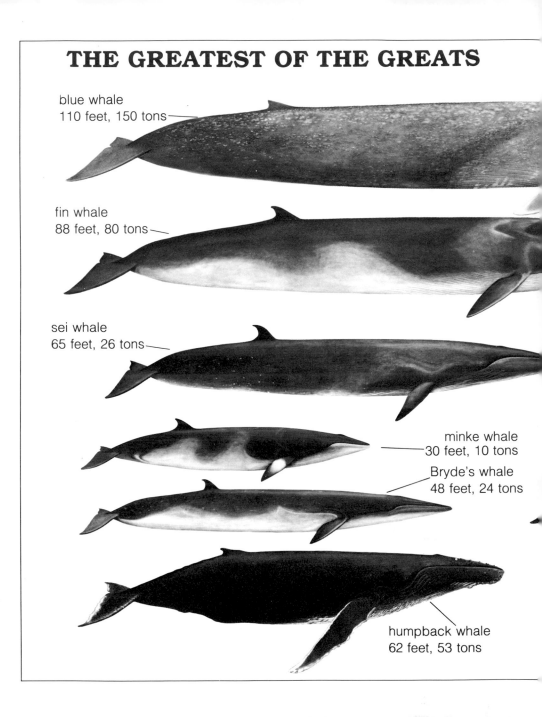

blue whale
110 feet, 150 tons

fin whale
88 feet, 80 tons

sei whale
65 feet, 26 tons

minke whale
30 feet, 10 tons

Bryde's whale
48 feet, 24 tons

humpback whale
62 feet, 53 tons

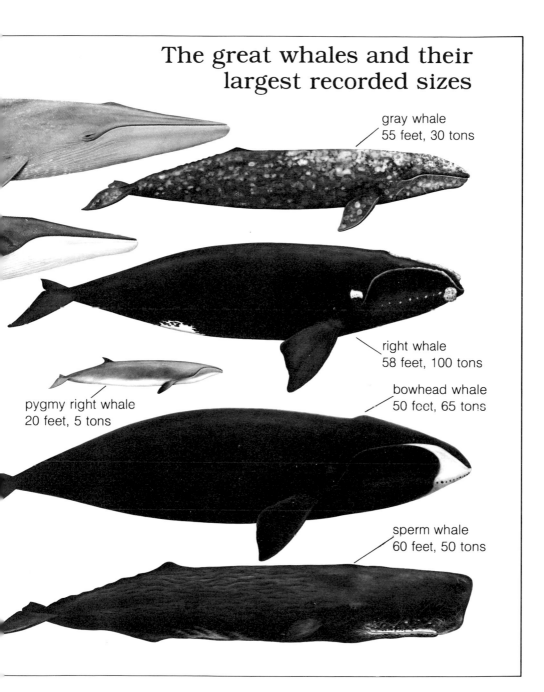

The great whales and their largest recorded sizes

gray whale
55 feet, 30 tons

right whale
58 feet, 100 tons

bowhead whale
50 feet, 65 tons

pygmy right whale
20 feet, 5 tons

sperm whale
60 feet, 50 tons

around ships and boats and may ride waves off a ship's bow.

The humpback is also a rorqual. But except for its pleated throat it does not look much like the others. It is a big whale with a chunky body, knobs on its head, and the longest flippers of any whale.

A second family of baleen whales has only one member, the gray whale. Grays are the only baleen whales that feed on the ocean floor. A gray whale swims along on its side. It sucks in a mouthful of water and small animals. Sometimes it rinses its mouth with clear water at the surface before swallowing its catch. Often it also swallows sand, stones, and seaweed.

The third family is made up of northern and southern right whales, the bowhead whale, and the pygmy right whale.

Right whales are fat, stocky animals with big flippers and huge lower lips that cover their baleen. They are slow swimmers.

Bowheads are also stocky animals. Like the

right whales, they feed by swimming through masses of tiny sea animals with their mouths open. Bowheads live only in Arctic waters.

The pygmy right whale is the smallest of all the great whales. It has been seen only in the Southern Hemisphere. Little is known about it.

No great whales are easy to study. Yet scientists have been able to learn a great deal about some of them.

3 ∥ Some Surprising Discoveries

Whales are mammals of the sea. People are mammals of the land. Scientists who study great whales cannot live among them. They cannot follow them on deep dives. They cannot travel far with them. And great whales are too big to capture and study.

For years, most of the whales that scientists studied were dead ones. Some had been killed by whale hunters. Some were found dead on beaches. The studies told scientists about the size and weight of whales, about their bodies. But they did not tell how whales live— where they go, what they do, and how they do it.

Someday scientists hope to learn about

Scientists sometimes swim with whales to study them. This humpback was netted, measured, and then released to go on its way.

whales by using satellites. Many wild animals have been tracked and studied in this way. Each animal wears a small package that gives off a radio signal. The signal is picked up by weather satellites and beamed to the ground. Experiments show that whales can also be tracked in this way. The signals show where they go and at what speed, how often and how deep they dive, how long they rest.

At present most studies of great whales are done by scientists in small boats. They spend days floating among groups of whales and even swimming with them.

Because they are close to the whales, scientists have learned how to tell one whale from another. They see and photograph scars, blotches, and other markings. In this way, they can tell if they are seeing the same whale year after year—or several whales. They can tell males from females. They can tell if groups stay together or change. They can track a whale and find out what it does.

HUMPBACK WHALES

To tell one humpback from another, scientists need to see the underside of the tail. All whales lift their tails when they are about to dive. A humpback's tail has black-and-white markings on the underside, on the broad end called the flukes. No two humpbacks have the same markings, just as no two people have the same fingerprints. By comparing photographs, scientists are learning how humpbacks live.

Some scientists have been studying humpbacks of the North Pacific. These whales spend the winter in warm waters off Hawaii or Baja California. They spend the summer some 3,000 miles to the north.

Some of the humpbacks feed alone. Some feed in small groups and work together. If they are feeding on krill, they may line up side by side and swim through the krill. Members of these groups often change. Small groups also work together to feed on schools of herring. The whales dive and circle the fish. They let air out of their lungs, forming a curtain of bubbles around the herring. The fish pack together inside the curtain. Then the whales shoot to the surface, passing through the fish with their mouths open. Members of these groups do not change. The same whales stay together, and they may work together summer after summer.

Humpbacks form herds when they are in their feeding grounds. Each herd has its own area, and the whales of one herd do not mingle with whales of another. Some scientists think that each herd is made up of groups of relatives. When the humpbacks swim south, the herd breaks up. Whales do not always winter in the same place. A humpback may spend one winter off Baja California and the next off Hawaii.

The warmer waters are where females bear their calves and where mating takes place. Here the males compete for females. Scientists often see a mother-calf pair being trailed by a male.

When breaching, a humpback hurls itself out of the water, twists in mid-air, and then lands with the crash of thunder.

Humpbacks often slap their flippers or flukes against the water.

No two humpbacks have the same markings on their flukes.

time. And the song changes every year. Humpbacks are usually alone when they sing. Often they are head down in the water, but they also sing at the surface.

Why do humpbacks sing? What do the songs mean? No one knows. In fact, no one even knows how they sing. Unlike us, they don't breathe out when singing.

RIGHT WHALES

Both northern and southern right whales are born with horny growths on their heads. The growths form a pattern, and no two patterns are alike. Photographs of the patterns are used by scientists who are studying how right whales behave and where they go. They are also trying to learn the meaning of the right whale's calls—grunts and growls and warbling sounds that the whales make both underwater and in the air.

Southern right whales spend the summer feeding in the Antarctic. They move to warmer waters for calving, raising their young, and mating. One of the places they are found is in the quiet bays of Patagonia, which is part of Argentina. By winter the bays are full of whales, breaching, spy-hopping, and slapping the water with their tails. On a windy day, a whale may raise its tail, use its flukes as a sail, and let the wind push it along. The snorts and gargles and splashes of whales can be heard ashore. Sometimes, when the whales are sleeping at the surface, they snore.

Most whales tumble through the water when they sleep. They may even hit bottom before rising again to breathe. But right whales are so fat that they float easily. They often sleep at the surface, looking like big logs. On calm days they may sleep so long that their backs become sunburned and peel. A sleeping right whale may also fall forward, with its head underwater and its tail in the air. From time to

No two right whales have the same pattern of horny growths on their heads. This right whale's open mouth shows its baleen.

time, the head comes up and the whale breathes.

Some of the whales are mothers with new-born calves. Each calf swims beside its mother's eye. From time to time, the mother pats the calf with her flipper. A hungry calf will butt its mother and climb on her, trying to get her to roll onto her side and nurse. A playful calf may keep banging into its mother or breaching onto her back. If the mother loses patience, she uses a flipper to hold the calf underwater. When it begins to sputter and cough, she lets it up. Or she may roll over on her back and cradle the calf on her chest, holding it with her flippers. Whatever happens, the two stay close together.

WHALE BIRTHS

Scientists would like to know more about the way great whales are born. They have seen the birth of dolphins in aquariums. These young are born near the surface, and they are born tail first. As soon as the baby is free, the mother or a friend helps it to the surface. There the baby starts to breathe. Because the baby is born head last, there is little danger that it will try to breathe underwater.

A few lucky scientists have caught sight of great whales giving birth at sea. It was hard to see exactly what happened. But the babies were born underwater and helped quickly to the surface. That was what scientists expected. Now they have found that gray whales, at least, may be different. One scientist saw and photographed a gray whale giving birth in a lagoon. The mother was lying on her back at the surface. Her baby was being born headfirst, with its head in the air. As soon as the baby was free of its mother, she helped to hold it up. Soon it was swimming on its own.

SPERM WHALES

Other scientists saw a sperm whale that was giving birth. One scientist dove in to see the baby. She reported that its tail flukes were bent toward its back. Its flippers rested in dents in its sides. The scientist was surprised to see that the baby had bright blue eyes, because other whales have dark eyes. As she watched, four other adult whales arrived and lifted the baby to the surface.

Sperm whales are very hard to study. These big toothed whales spend their time in deep waters and cannot be studied from a base camp on land. Also, much of their time is spent diving for food. They dive so deep that scientists cannot follow them.

Some sperm whales seem to live alone, but many live in groups of about 25. In winter the groups are made up of young whales and their mothers, other females, and one or two big males. The females and young form long-lasting groups, while the big males move from group to group. Also, in summer the males, young and old, go off to feed in cold seas. Females and their calves stay in warmer waters.

Sperm whales seem to like company. When they are not diving, they seek each other out. They may swim together or float together at the surface. They often nuzzle or gently stroke one another with their flippers.

In many ways, sperm whales are the most mysterious of all whales. They can dive as deep as a mile and stay down for 40 to 60 minutes. How can their bodies stand the pressure? No one is sure. At those depths, there is no light. Yet sperm whales find and feed on giant squid. How do they do it? Scientists think they know part of the answer, but only part.

Sperm whales send out great bursts of clicking noises—about one click a second. When the clicks strike something, they echo back to the whales. It seems likely that the whales use the echoes to find their way in the dark and to find food—that the echo from a giant squid does not sound like the echo from a rock. But just how they tell is not known. Nor does anyone know how the whales send out the clicks.

All whales have big brains. But the sperm whale has the biggest brain of any creature that has ever lived. Why does it have such a big brain? What does it use the big brain for?

The forehead of a sperm whale holds a large amount of oil that is slightly waxy when cool. No one knows for certain why the whale has this oil. But scientists suspect that the oil and big brain play an important part in the way that a sperm whale sends out clicks and receives echoes.

Like other great whales, the sperm whale seems to have only one enemy in the sea. This is the 20-foot-long orca, or killer whale. Its bites can be seen in the flukes of many whales. But a group of sperm whales can defend itself from orcas.

Several scientists were studying sperm whales and listening to their clicks when the whales suddenly fell silent. A pack of orcas was circling the sperm whales. The sperm whales stayed close together and turned to face outward. Now they began clicking loudly.

For three hours the orcas circled, trying to get behind the sperm whales. For three hours

WHALE BLOWS

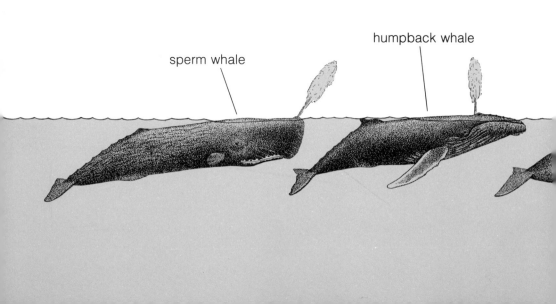

humpback whale

sperm whale

the sperm whales kept their tails and bodies in and their great square heads out. They kept one small calf at the center of their group, well away from the orcas. Finally the closely packed sperm whales began turning in a tight circle, revolving once every two or three minutes. The orcas gave up and swam away. Now the sperm

A sperm whale has a single blowhole. The blowhole is tilted forward and so is the blow. Baleen whales have two blowholes. Their blows have different sizes and shapes. A whale watcher with experience can tell one kind of whale from another by the look of the blow.

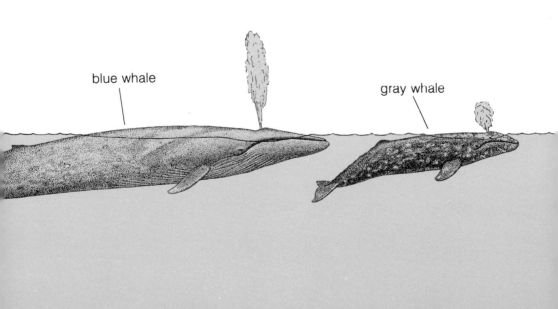

blue whale

gray whale

whales fell silent. They, too, swam away, traveling fast at seven miles an hour. By morning they were 85 miles from where the orcas had tried to attack them.

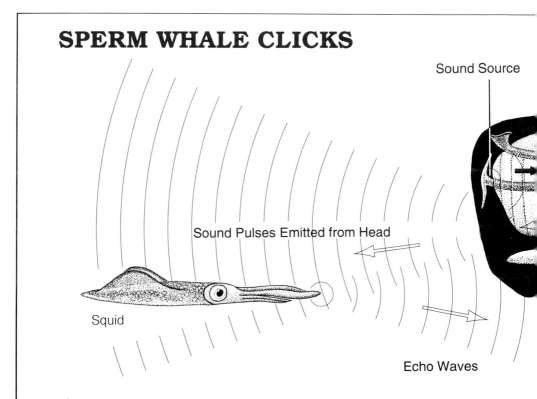

SPERM WHALE CLICKS

Sound Source

Sound Pulses Emitted from Head

Squid

Echo Waves

Sperm whales make noises that sound like bangs to our ears. Each bang is really a burst of very fast clicks. No one knows for sure how the clicks are made. But some scientists think they start with an explosion of air near the front of the whale's snout. The noise rockets

Orcas are a sometimes deadly enemy of great whales. But over the years human beings have done far more harm to the great whales than all the orcas in the world.

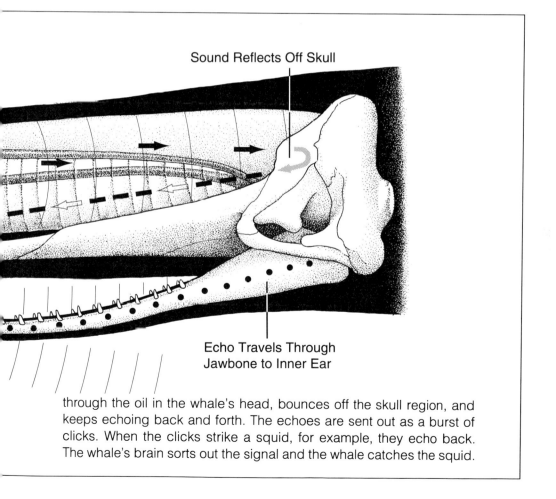

Sound Reflects Off Skull

Echo Travels Through Jawbone to Inner Ear

through the oil in the whale's head, bounces off the skull region, and keeps echoing back and forth. The echoes are sent out as a burst of clicks. When the clicks strike a squid, for example, they echo back. The whale's brain sorts out the signal and the whale catches the squid.

4 ∥ *The Whale Hunters*

For at least a thousand years, people have been hunting whales. At first whalers hunted from land, setting out in small boats when they saw whales blowing offshore. Sometimes they drove whales ashore. Sometimes they speared whales with harpoons and towed them a-shore. Later whalers took to the sea and sailed along coasts. When they spotted whales, they launched small boats. Men in the boats har-pooned whales and towed them back to the ships or to whaling stations on shore.

Over time the number of whales swimming near shore grew smaller and smaller. Ships grew bigger. They sailed into deeper waters to hunt whales. They sailed away from home for weeks or months at a time.

In those early days, whaling was danger-

Modern ships and harpoons tipped with explosives let whale hunters pursue, kill, and process giants of the ocean, such as fin whales.

In the 1700s and 1800s, men set out in 30-foot capture boats to harpoon sperm whales that were 60 feet long and weighed 50 tons. It was dangerous work.

ous. The boats were small. The whales were big—and they fought when attacked. Many boats were crushed or overturned. Even ships were sunk. Hunters feared great whales, but they thought the prize was worth the danger.

Some peoples hunted whales as food. All hunted whales for oil and baleen. The oil came from blubber that had been heated and melted down. Whale oil fueled the lamps of the world. Baleen stiffened everything from clothing to umbrellas and fishing rods. By the early 1800s oil from the sperm whale was being used to make margarine and soap. Oil from its head went into candles and later into lipsticks, rouge, crayons, pencils, and other products.

By the late 1800s people were using oil from the ground to light their lamps. And soon electricity took the place of oil. New uses were found for whale oil, and the hunting went on. But the battle between whales and whalers changed. New whaling ships of the 1900s were made of steel and run by engines. Powerful cannons fired harpoons tipped with explosives. Giant ships could haul giant whales aboard, turn blubber into oil and bones into fertilizer. The great whales no longer had a chance.

Finally a number of scientists became alarmed. They feared that some kinds of great whales would soon be wiped out. In the 1940s meetings were held, and whaling countries agreed to stop hunting some kinds of great whales. Still, scientists went on worrying, as

In earlier days whales were hauled ashore to be stripped of blubber, baleen, and other parts. This one is a bowhead, also known as a Greenland whale.

well as studying and counting whales. It was only in 1986 that the worst of the killing stopped. Most whaling countries then agreed to stop or nearly stop hunting. A few peoples, such as Eskimos, who depend on the sea for food, were allowed to hunt small numbers of whales.

An 1858 advertisement tells of whale products that were for sale.

Yet between 1900 and 1986 a million and a half great whales were killed. Some kinds are still in danger, because their numbers are small. They may not have enough young to make up for older whales that die.

Right whales were heavily hunted from the beginning. Slow moving, they swam near shore, floated when killed, and yielded large amounts of oil and baleen. In fact, that is why they are called right whales. To whalers they were "right" whales to kill. Almost no one has hunted right whales for nearly 50 years. Yet their numbers remain small. Scars show that many have been injured by ships or fishing gear.

Bowheads once swam in nearly all Arctic waters. They were much hunted for 300 years. Now they are seen in only a few places.

Gray whales used to live in both the Atlantic and Pacific oceans in the Northern Hemisphere. Whaling wiped them out in the Atlantic and part of the Pacific. Like the right whales, they were easy to hunt, because they swam near land. They were easy to find, because they swam the same route every year. At two different times, gray whales of the eastern Pacific almost disappeared. Each time, they made a comeback. Today they are great whales that seem to be doing well.

Among the rorquals, humpbacks were heavily hunted for many years. Like the right whales and grays, they swam along coasts. They could be hunted from land stations and also at sea. So far they have not made a real comeback.

Fast steamships and harpoons with explosives let whalers hunt blue whales. In a fairly short time, they killed more than 90 percent of all the blue whales in the Southern Hemisphere. Today only a small population is left, and it does not seem to be growing. Most blue whales are in the Northern Hemisphere.

As blues grew harder to find, whalers turned to fin whales. As the fin whales grew harder to find, whalers turned to sei whales and then to minkes.

Sperm whales have been much hunted, although many of them still swim the oceans. But whalers went after older males, which were giant in size. Scientists now wonder how the taking of older males has affected the herds. They wonder if it affects breeding and the number of young that are born.

Will the great whales survive? Right now, no one can say. If there is little hunting, that will help. But there are other problems too. Humans have been polluting the oceans for years. Pollution can destroy the feeding and calving grounds of whales. That is why some scientists are trying hard to find out where whales go. They hope to protect the food supplies of whales. They hope to protect the quiet places where whales give birth to their young.

The story of mankind and the great whales is not a pretty one. But there is hope it will yet have a happy ending, for people can change their minds and change their ways. Today, in many parts of the world, people are working to save the whales, to keep them from being hunted. They are learning about whales, getting to know them. And sometimes they reach out to help whales in trouble.

Harpooner stands ready in the bow as a capture boat nears a sperm whale.

5 ∥ A Race Against Time

There were three of them, three young gray whales. They had been feeding off the coast of northern Alaska, near the Eskimo settlement of Barrow. And they had stayed too long. Winter comes early to the Arctic. It may also come quickly, as it did in the fall of 1988, with a sudden drop in temperature. The sea froze. Ice formed all around the whales. There were only two openings where they could surface and breathe.

An Eskimo discovered the whales on October 7. He saw at once what had happened.

News of the trapped whales spread quickly. Government scientists rushed to Barrow. So did scientists from companies that were pumping oil in the far north. All wanted to help the whales, but helping was not going to be easy.

One of the trapped gray whales raises its head out of the ice.

The sea ice was anchored to the land and not about to blow away. Worse yet, the way to open water was blocked by a huge ridge of ice. With winter beginning, the rescue became a race against time.

The best hope was an oil barge that wasn't far away. Perhaps it could be used as an ice-breaker to smash through a narrow part of the ridge. If so, it would open up a path leading to open water. Meanwhile, the holes had to be kept open so that the whales could breathe.

Eskimos and other men set to work, bundled up against the bitter cold. They cut out blocks of ice with chain saws. They used poles to push the blocks under the sea ice. In this way, they made the holes larger. They were interested to see that the whales moved easily from one hole to another. No one understood how the whales could do this—find their way between two holes that were a hundred yards apart.

Day after day the men worked on the holes.

They felt they were getting to know the whales and gave them names: Bonnet, Cross, and Bone.

By October 19 the weather was worse. Blowing snow was filling the holes and the men couldn't keep them open. Just in time two men flew in from Minnesota. They had heard about the whales and thought they could help. With them they brought machines called de-icers. Each de-icer was made of an electric motor and a propeller inside a wire cage. The motor ran the propeller. The propeller stirred up the water and brought warmer water from below. The warmer water kept the holes open.

A de-icer was placed in one of the holes. The whales were curious, not frightened. A second de-icer was placed in the other hole. The whales moved to that hole. They seemed to like the de-icers, and that gave the men an idea.

Perhaps they could make a series of holes leading toward a narrow part of the ice ridge. They could use de-icers to attract the whales to the new holes. That way the whales would be near the place where the oil barge was going to break through.

Bad news arrived. The oil barge wasn't coming. It was stuck in ice and could not be freed. Even so, it still seemed a good idea to move the whales toward the narrow part of the ridge. The work went on. Eskimos took the lead, working long hours with chain saws and poles to make new holes. The whales moved. The plan was working. But in the excitement there was also sadness. Bone, the youngest whale, was missing. Scientists thought Bone had probably become lost under the ice when the whales moved.

More equipment poured in—poles, floodlights, generators to make electricity. The hours of daylight were short now. Then the whales stopped moving. Everyone was puzzled. The new holes had water 12 feet deep, which seemed enough. As the men wondered what to do, some good news arrived.

Eskimos use poles to push freshly cut slabs of ice under the solid ice.

The United States government had talked to the Soviet government. The Soviets were sending two icebreakers that had been working in the Arctic. Now there was no need to lead Bonnet and Cross through shallow water to a narrow part of the ice ridge. The icebreakers could crunch through any part of it. The next new holes were made in slightly deeper water— and the whales moved. Scientists realized that

Bonnet and Cross spy-hop in an open track of water.

the whales had feared the shallow water. "We just didn't understand what they were trying to tell us," one said.

On October 25 and 26 the icebreakers chopped a huge opening in the ice ridge. The men working on the ice were excited and hopeful. They felt the whales knew they were being led to open water. The smaller icebreaker now made a run through the sea ice. It opened a track to a whale hole. The whales entered the track. But as darkness fell, everyone could see that the going was rough. The water was full of floating chunks of ice.

Long before the sun rose on October 27, Eskimos were out on the ice. They found Bonnet and Cross had traveled about a mile and a half in the right direction. The whales were keeping afloat in a small opening. But they had scraped and cut themselves on chunks of ice.

With broken ice all around, there was nothing firm to stand on. It was hard for the men to work near the whales. The weather was worse. Time was growing short. That night they left the whales with a de-icer, and left a floodlight to guide the icebreaker.

The next morning Bonnet and Cross were seen starting down the new track made by the icebreaker. Deep open water lay ahead of them. With luck they would soon be swimming south to Baja California.

Index

Boldface indicates picture.